Favorite
REDWORK DESIGNS

Betty Alderman

American Quilter's Society

P. O. Box 3290 • Paducah, KY 42002-3290

Located in Paducah, Kentucky, the American Quilter's Society (AQS) is dedicated to promoting the accomplishments of today's quilters. Through its publications and events, AQS strives to honor today's quiltmakers and their work and to inspire future creativity and innovation in quiltmaking.

EDITOR: SHELLEY HAWKINS
TECHNICAL EDITOR: BARBARA SMITH
BOOK DESIGN/ILLUSTRATIONS: ELAINE WILSON
COVER DESIGN: MICHAEL BUCKINGHAM
PHOTOGRAPHY: CHARLES R. LYNCH

Library of Congress Cataloging-in-Publication Data
Alderman, Betty
     Favorite redwork designs / Betty Alderman.
        p. cm.
     Includes bibliographical references.
     ISBN 1-574-32733-X
     1. Quilting--Patterns. 2. Appliqué--Patterns. 3.Embroidery--Patterns I. Title.

TT835.A43 1999
746.46'041--dc21   99-040081

Additional copies of this book may be ordered from the American Quilter's Society, PO Box 3290, Paducah, KY 42002-3290, or online at www.AQSquilt.com.

Dedication

I have known my husband since I was four years old. He came to my birthday party that year and has been in the picture ever since. Because we have such a long history together, he has always known where I was coming from.

This book is for you, Fred, because you are everything to me, and you seem to think everything I do is worthy of your praises.

Acknowledgments

It is said that no one can create in a vacuum. I am reminded of that every day as I try to find inspiration for the work I do. Without the stimulation derived from my friends and family, I would never have put pen to paper; would never have threaded a needle; or thought about publishing my ideas for needlework. Thank you all.

I thank my mother, Ada Waples, who sewed a fine seam and taught me the pleasures of striving to do the same. I can still hear her saying, "I did the best I could."

Betsy Lewis, my daughter, knows her way around a computer and is so generous with all her knowledge. Thank you, Betsy.

Diane Ebner, machine quilter extraordinaire, quilted most of the quilts in this book. Thank you for making my embroidered quilt tops become the quilts I am proud to include in this book.

To my friend, Katie Goetzmann, thank you for helping me with the embroidery. I can just picture all of the floss hanging from the visor of your car as you and Don were driving to Florida! Many people can't stitch in a car. I'm so glad you can.

Laurene Sinema has, perhaps more than anyone, encouraged me to go after my dream of creating quilts that other people might enjoy making. Thank you, Laurene, for believing in me. Laurene owns the Quilted Apple in Phoenix, Arizona. She has always had the most unbelievable staff in her shop. I thank all of those wonderful people for their friendship and the encouragement they have given me over the years.

I might never have sold my first pattern if it had not been for Janet Williams, owner of the Quilt Connection in Mansfield, Ohio. Thanks to you, Janet, I'm still at it. Janet is also part of the Tuesday Quilt Club in Mansfield. They were, and are, a wonderful support group for me.

Now I am back in my hometown of Palmyra, New York, and I am part of a circle of friends who love to do handwork. Some are embroiders, some are knitters, and some are quilters. We meet every Thursday and are there for each other, no matter what our needs. That is really what this page of acknowledgments is about. Thank you all for being there.

Last but not least, I thank Meredith Schroeder and all the AQS staff — Barbara Smith, Shelley Hawkins, Elaine Wilson, Michael Buckingham, Charles R. Lynch, Bonnie Browning, and Helen Squire — for their belief in me and for allowing me to be part of the AQS group of authors. It has truly been a pleasure.

Contents

BOTANICAL REDWORK

40" x 46"

Favorite Redwork Designs / Betty Alderman

Introduction

One of my earliest memories is of my mother, on hands and knees, helping me find the needle I had dropped on the living room carpet. I couldn't have been more than five years old, but she was teaching me to ply my needle on some of my first handwork.

In those days, colorful embroidery was in vogue and I learned to make lazy daisies, tiny French knots, and almost-straight stem stitches, using a variety of colorful floss worked on stamped squares from the five & dime store. I don't know what happened to those early attempts at needle art, but I imagine my mother saved them for years, tucked away in her attic with all my other unfinished projects.

As I grew older, I embroidered pillowcases, hand towels, luncheon cloths, and napkins. Inevitably, my interests broadened to other types of needlework, such as knitting, needlepoint, cross-stitch embroidery, and eventually, quiltmaking.

Somewhere along the line, I fell in love with antique quilts and have spent many happy hours at auctions, searching for old quilts. My heart begins to beat wildly each time a quilt comes on the block. Will it be mine? How much do I dare spend? On several occasions, I have been lucky enough to be the high bidder on a redwork quilt. The crisp red and white color scheme and fanciful designs hold great appeal for me. I am reminded of those stamped squares my mother bought me years ago. Redwork was past its prime when I was learning to embroider. However, had it been as popular during the '40s as it was in the early part of the century, I know I would have been a devotee, as red, any red, was, and is, my favorite color.

I love red leather shoes, woolly red mittens, shiny red apples, cherry red lipstick, and waxy red crayons. I even have red counter tops in my kitchen! Red combined with white is even better. Red and white checks, red and white ticking, candy canes, and most of all, red and white quilts make my spirits soar.

The designs in this book are new, but my inspiration came from designs found on old redwork quilts. Flowers and garden tools were popular embroidery motifs, as were Sunbonnet figures. We often find letters of the alphabet worked in red, too.

Blue was a popular choice for early single-color embroidered quilts. Any of the designs found among these pages would be charming worked in blue or any favorite color you choose. Some of the quilts in this book have been worked in a combination of colors. By all means, experiment. There is no right color. I know of a little girl who told her grandma she wanted to make a purplework quilt and then proceeded to do so. Pick your color, and stitch away. Try mixing the designs to create your own unique quilt. I'm sure you will love the results.

Using this Book

People who love redwork seem to have an insatiable appetite for patterns to embroider. Within these pages, I have added more than 80 designs to their storehouses of redwork motifs. These designs have been stitched into eight different projects. Some projects, such as the tea towels, can be completed in just a few hours, while others will take somewhat longer.

Supplies to Have on Hand

The supplies listed in this section are needed to complete the projects in this book. Additional items are listed with the directions for each individual project.

One of the first rules student artists and craftsmen learn is to use the very best tools they can afford. It is much easier to do good work if you begin with superior materials and equipment. Needles should be the right size, scissors should be sharp and pointed, and embroidery hoops should hold the fabric taut. The fabric itself should be of the highest quality. Remembering this rule will make you a happy stitcher.

TOOLS

- Extra hard pencil or fine line permanent pen
- Embroidery needles, size 7 or 8
- Embroidery hoop, 6"
- Thimble
- All-purpose thread for piecing quilts
- Embroidery scissors

FABRIC

Antique redwork embroidery was traditionally done on white fabric. If another fabric was added as sashing or borders, it was usually solid red or blue. Now, 100 years or more after the first redwork quilts were made, let your imagination be your guide when choosing fabrics for your embroidery. The background does not always have to be solid white, although that is certainly an appropriate choice. Quilt shops carry a wide selection of white-on-white muslin as well as a variety of wonderful light shirtings with just a hint of a pattern in them. Light background fabrics can range from pure white to tea-dyed tans. Consider the other fabrics you will be using in your projects when choosing your background fabrics. When combined, will the light background fabric work well with the other chosen prints or solids? Remember, for a traditional look, combine white with solid red or blue. For a newer look, try the beautiful prints we now have available to us.

Always choose 100% cotton fabrics. Do not be tempted to use cotton sheeting because the high thread count will make it difficult to stitch. Prewash your fabrics before you begin. This will allow you to check for color fastness and eliminate chances of too much shrinkage. Dry fabrics in the dryer and press. *Hint: I find the needle slips through the fabric a little easier if I spray starch lightly when pressing.*

TEA TOWELS

Several of the designs in this book are embroidered on tea towels. Use high-quality towels, and they will be a beautiful showcase for your embroidery. Refer to the Sources section, page 94, for stores where the towels can be purchased.

THREAD

DMC® cotton embroidery floss is the thread I recommend for embroidery. The quality and colors are consistent and reliable. People often question the chance of the red floss running or bleeding. The following steps can be taken to test your floss:

- Wet several strands of floss with warm water.
- Place the wet strands on a scrap of white fabric.
- With the floss still on the fabric, press both with a warm iron.

If bleeding occurs, soak the skein of floss in a glass of water. Continue changing the water until it remains clear.

General Directions

Please read through each pattern's directions before you begin to cut or stitch. All seam allowances are ¼" and are included in the cutting measurements. Although every effort has been made to make these directions as clear and precise as possible, it is assumed that the needle artist using this book is familiar with basic quiltmaking techniques.

Cut background blocks about 1" larger than the measurements given. After the embroidery is complete, press the block, face down, on a Turkish towel, and then trim to the correct size.

The lengths given for sashings and bor-ders are the ideal measurements. If this were a perfect world, you could rely on them. However, individual quilts may vary. I suggest you measure your quilt as you piece it together to determine the exact length you need to cut your sashings and borders.

Two quilts contain setting triangles, SUN-BONNET FLOWER SHOW – REDWORK QUILT and FRIENDS AT MY GARDEN GATE. Triangles have a habit of shrinking after they have been sewn into a quilt. Therefore, the triangle measurements given are slightly larger than re-quired. Trim the triangles to size after they have been applied to the quilt.

Transferring Your Designs to Fabric

There are several methods for transferring your chosen design to your background fabric. The two methods I prefer are the tracing method and the light box and pen method. Directions for both are shown here.

TRACING METHOD: This is the method you will probably use most often.

Place your light background fabric, face up, over the desired design.

Trace the design with an extra hard pencil or fine line permanent pen. The advantage of a pencil is that it will erase if you make a mistake. The advantage of a pen is that it is easier to use on fabrics that don't have a perfectly smooth surface, such as the Jacquard tea towels.

The following light box and pen method suggests making a photocopy of the design you want to transfer to fabric. Permission is granted to make these copies for the purpose of transferring the designs to fabric for your own personal use.

LIGHT BOX AND PEN METHOD: This method works well on denser fabrics or slightly textured fabrics, such as the Jacquard tea towels.

- Make a copy of the desired designs by tracing or making a photocopy.
- Place the copy on top of a light box and place the background fabric or towel, right-side up, on top of the tracing or copy.
- Trace the design, using a fine line permanent pen. The pen should be the same color as the floss you intend to use.
- Heat-set the pen tracing with a medium-hot iron.

Embroidery Stitches

The following stitches are used throughout this book.

Fig. 1. Stem Stitch

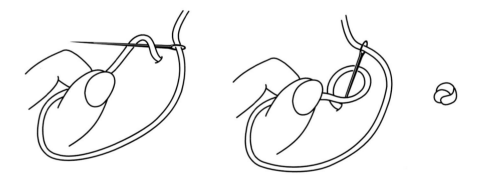

Fig. 2. French Knot

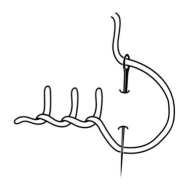

Fig. 3. Buttonhole Stitch

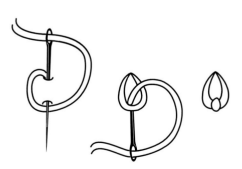

Fig. 4. Lazy Daisy

Hints for Doing Superior Embroidery

- Always wash your hands before you begin to stitch.
- Pull about 18" of floss from the skein and cut.
- Strip one strand at a time from the 18" length. Do this by grasping the length of floss with your left hand, near the top. With your right hand, grasp one strand and pull up, separating it from the rest. Repeat with each strand you will be using (Fig. 5).
- Only knot your thread when you begin to embroider a new design. After that, whenever starting a new thread, run it under several stitches on the back and do the same when you have finished with that thread. This will lessen the chance of your thread showing through on the front.
- You should not allow your thread to travel more than about ¼" on the back of your work. Otherwise, it will probably show through the fabric. If you need to stop and start again, further than ¼", you can run your thread under several stitches to get to the new starting place.
- When using a hoop, remove it each time you set your work aside to eliminate a ring showing up on your work after it is complete.

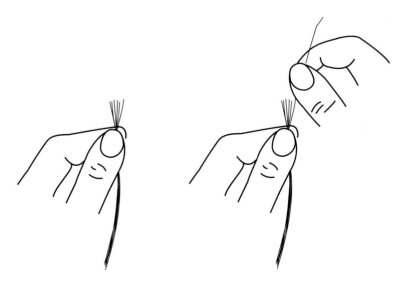

Fig. 5. Separation of Floss

Finishing Your Quilt

Press your completed quilt top, face down, on a padded surface or Turkish towel. Make sure the seam allowances are pressed toward the darker fabric, if possible. Check for any stray threads that may show through the quilt top because they can be difficult to hide after the quilt top is basted.

Make a sandwich of your quilt top, batting, and backing by placing the backing face down, layering the batting on top of the backing, and placing the quilt top, face up, on top of the batting. Baste the three layers together. The batting and backing should extend beyond the quilt top by several inches. *Hint: I have tried quilt-basting spray on several small projects and find it works very well.* Refer to the Sources section, page 94, for locating quilt-basting spray.

Quilting

Many of the quilt projects pictured in this book have been machine quilted. Machine quilting has become an accepted method of finishing quilts and, in some instances, it enhances quilts beyond the limitations of hand quilting. If you decide to machine quilt your redwork project, use clear monofilament thread (for purchasing information, refer to the Sources section, page 94) when stitching so the thread won't show when stitched over the embroidery. If you are planning to hand quilt any of these projects, look to the designs themselves for quilt motif ideas. I hand quilted the CATNIP TEA PARTY quilt and used the teapots for a quilting design, adding swirls of steam coming from their spouts.

When the quilting is complete, trim away the excess batting and backing. Straighten the edges and square up the corners of the quilt.

Binding

Directions for binding all of the quilts, except the BOTANICAL REDWORK quilt.
- Cut or make 2 strips, 1⅛" x the width of the quilt, plus 5".
- Cut or make 2 strips, 1⅛" x the length of the quilt, plus 5".
- Center the binding strips on the sides of the quilt, right sides together and edges

matching. The strips will extend about 2½" beyond each end of the quilt.

- Start stitching ¼" in from the end of the quilt and stitch to within ¼" of the opposite end.

- After all 4 strips have been sewn, miter the corners (Fig. 6) and bring the binding to the back of the quilt.

- Turn the binding in ¼" and whipstitch in place (Fig. 7).

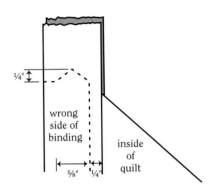
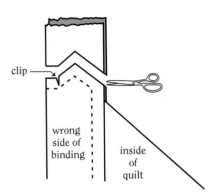

Fig. 6. Mitered Corner Diagram

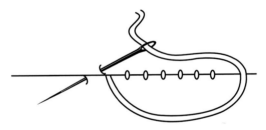

Fig. 7. Whipstitch

Binding the Botanical Redwork Quilt

- Make a bias binding 1⅛" x the circumference of the quilt, plus 5".
- Pin the binding to the quilt, right sides together and edges matching.
- Ease the binding around the curved corners.

- Stitch around the entire quilt. Trim away the excess binding and make a seam where the ends of the binding meet.
- Bring the binding to the back of the quilt, fold in ¼", and whipstitch in place (Fig. 7).

Redwork Projects

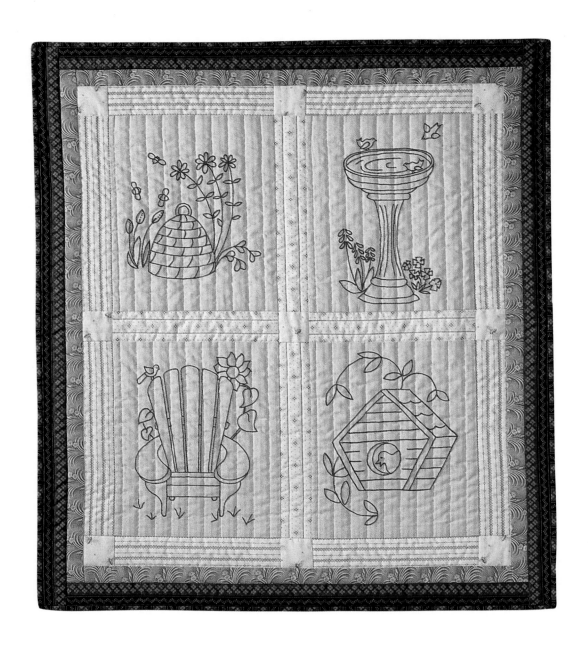

BIRDS AND THE BEES
28¼" x 32¼"

Favorite Redwork Designs / Betty Alderman

Birds and the Bees

When starting to work on this quilt, I was thinking of some of the things one might find in one's garden. It was going to be called FAVORITE THINGS, but as it evolved, the name was changed to BIRDS AND THE BEES. I think you can see why. There were birds in three of the designs and bees in the other, but the clincher was the corner-set fabric. It is a wonderful shirting print depicting beautifully etched bees. There are two borders on this quilt, although there appears to be three, because the outside border is a stripe.

SUPPLY LIST

- 3 skeins of DMC® floss, red 498
- ⅜ yd. light background fabric
- 1 fat quarter each of two different light prints for sashing
- ⅛ yd. light print for corner sets
- ¼ yd. medium print for inner border
- ½ yd. dark print for outer border and binding, cut across fabric or, if using a stripe, 1 yd. of dark print for outer border and binding, cut lengthwise
- 32" x 36" backing fabric
- 32" x 36" batting fabric

CUTTING MEASUREMENTS

BACKGROUND: Cut 4 rectangles, 9½" x 11½"

SASHING: Cut 6 strips, 2¼" x 11½"
Cut 6 strips, 2¼" x 9½"

Note: Cut the inside sashing from one of the fat quarters and the outside sashing from the other fat quarter.

CORNER SETS: Cut 9 squares, 2¼" x 2¼"

INNER BORDER: Cut 2 strips, 1½" x 23¾"
Cut 2 strips, 1½" x 29¾"

OUTER BORDER: Cut 2 strips, 2" x 25¾"
Cut 2 strips, 2" x 32¾"

DIRECTIONS

- Transfer the 4 BIRDS AND THE BEES designs to the background rectangles by the method you prefer. Refer to the Transferring Your Designs to Fabric section, page 10.
- Embroider the designs, using a stem stitch (Fig. 1, page 11) and 2 strands of floss.
- Assemble the quilt, using the BIRDS AND THE BEES layout guide (Fig. 8).
- Refer to the General Directions section, page 9, for finishing your quilt.

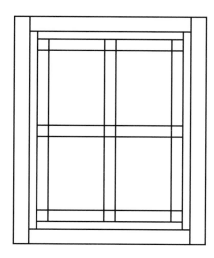

Fig. 8. BIRDS AND THE BEES Layout Guide

Birds and the Bees

• French knot

Favorite Redwork Designs / Betty Alderman

Birds and the Bees

French knot

French
knots

Favorite Redwork Designs / Betty Alderman

Birds and the Bees

French knot

CATNIP TEA PARTY

22½" x 22½"

Favorite Redwork Designs / Betty Alderman

Catnip Tea Party

A few years ago, I bought an autograph book that dated from the 1880s. I gave the book to a friend as a gift, but one of the verses has always remained in my mind:

"When this you see,
Remember me,
And take a little
Catnip Tea"

I knew that I would make a quilt someday as a reminder of that verse from long ago. I had been playing around with the design idea, for quite sometime, of two young ladies sharing tea on a sofa. I hope you like the results. The borders are made up of simple Nine-Patch blocks. I love the scrappy, postage-stamp look they create when placed side by side. Consider the teapots in the corners for other projects as well. I think they would look marvelous embroidered on tea towels.

SUPPLY LIST

- 1 skein each of the following DMC® floss:
    - Blue 796
    - Red 304
    - Pink 603
    - Medium green 987
    - Light green 704
    - Black 310
    - Lavender 208
    - Peach 722
    - Brown 938
- ½ yd. background fabric for embroidery
- Total of 12 fat quarters; 6 medium or dark prints and 6 light prints for the Nine-Patch border
- ¼ yd. plaid fabric for inner border
- 27" x 27" batting
- 27" x 27" backing
- ¼ yd. binding fabric

CUTTING MEASUREMENTS

NINE-PATCH BLOCKS: Cut 9 medium or dark strips, 18" x 2", from the medium and dark prints.
Cut 9 strips, 18" x 2", from the light prints.

BACKGROUND: Cut the center block 15" x 15". This will be trimmed to size after the embroidery is complete and the borders have been made.
Cut 4 corner squares, 5½" x 5½". These will be trimmed to size before being added to the borders.

INNER BORDER: Cut 4 border strips, 1" x the length required. The length will be determined after the center block and the Nine-Patch borders are complete.

DIRECTIONS

- Transfer the CATNIP TEA PARTY design to the background fabric by the method you prefer. Refer to the Transferring Your Designs to Fabric section, page 10.
- Transfer the 4 teapot designs to the 4 corner squares.
- Embroider the designs, using the stem stitch (Fig. 1, page 11) and 2 strands of floss, except on the faces, arms, and legs. Use 1 strand of floss on these.
- Sew 3 sets of 2 medium or dark and 1 light 18" x 2" print strips.
- Sew 3 sets of 2 light and 1 dark or medium 18" x 2" print strips (Fig. 9). Remember to vary each set.
- Cut these sets into 2" segments (Fig. 10).
- Make 12 Nine-Patch blocks. Eight of the blocks should have dark or medium corners, and 4 should have light corners (Fig. 11).
- Sew 4 border strips by sewing 3 Nine-Patch blocks together. The blocks with the darker corners will be on either end, and the blocks with the light corners will be in the middle. Ideally, the borders will measure 14" long after they are sewn. If they are shorter don't be concerned.
- In all cases, trim your center block to measure ½" less than the length of your Nine-Patch borders. In other words, if the borders measure 14" long, cut the center block 13½" square. If the borders measure 13½" long, cut the center block 13" square, and so on.

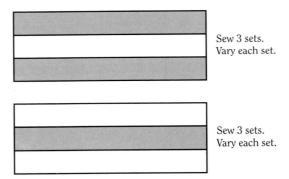

Sew 3 sets.
Vary each set.

Sew 3 sets.
Vary each set.

Fig. 9. Varying Strips Diagram

Make 8.

Make 4.

Fig. 11. Nine-Patch Blocks

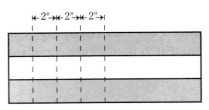

Cut into 2" segments.

Fig. 10. 2" Segments Diagram

Favorite Redwork Designs / Betty Alderman

- Cut 2 inner border strips, 1" x the width of your center block.
- Sew the inner border strips to the top and bottom of the center block.
- Cut 2 inner border strips, 1" x the length of the center block, plus the top and bottom inner borders.

- Sew these strips to the sides of the center block.
- Trim the teapot corner blocks to the exact size of the Nine-Patch blocks.
- Finish assembling the quilt according to the CATNIP TEA PARTY layout guide (Fig. 12).

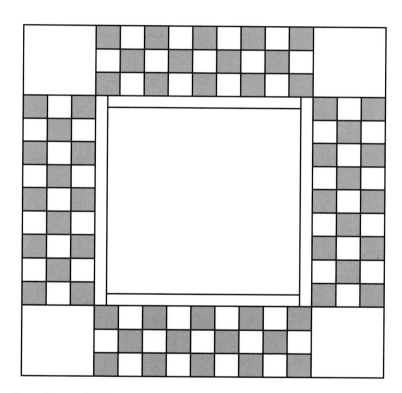

Fig. 12. CATNIP TEA PARTY Layout Guide

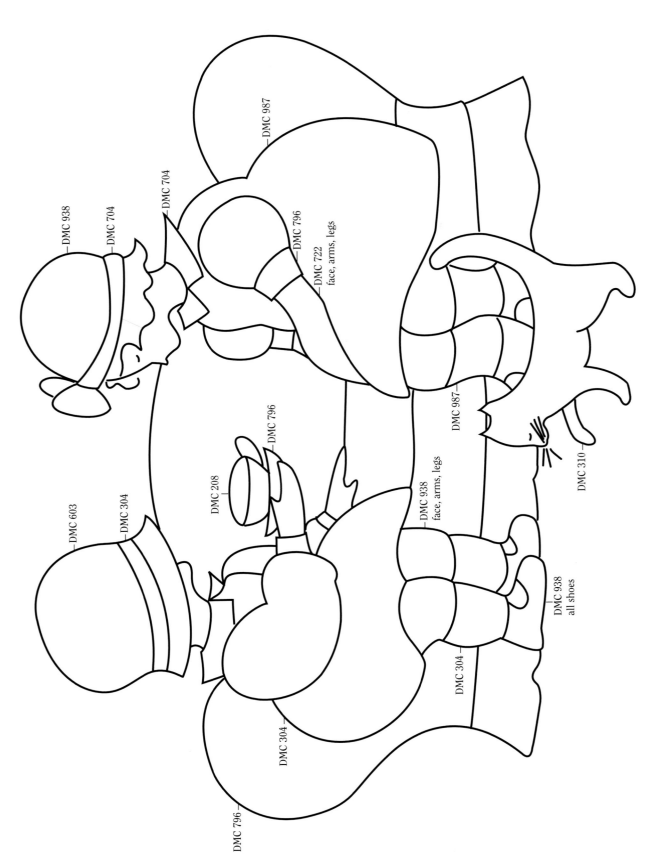

Catnip Tea Party and Tea Towel Fun

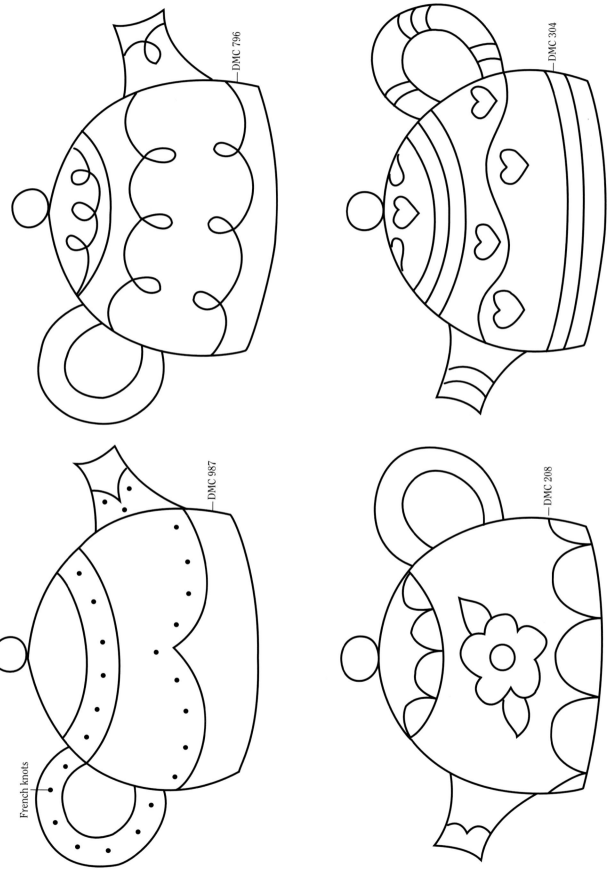

DMC 796

DMC 304

DMC 987

DMC 208

French knots

BLUE TEA POTS

RED TEA CUPS

GREEN GARDEN COLLAGE

Favorite Redwork Designs / Betty Alderman

Tea Towel Fun

Tea towels have been embellished with embroidery for many years. Visit an antique shop and you will most likely find examples of embroidered towels dating from Victorian times right up through the 1950s. In my collection of redwork, there is an example of a lovely Jacquard towel embroidered in red, depicting elaborate cutlery. Look around the housewares section in department stores and shops and you will find a variety of Jacquard towels just begging to have a touch of embroidery added. The word "Jacquard" refers to the name of the inventor of the loom on which these lovely, multicolored towels are woven. It is the same type of loom that was used to weave the beautiful coverlets of the last century that are so prized by collectors today.

Days of the week and Sunbonnets enhanced plainer towels of the '40s and '50s. Among my favorites from that time period are a series of towels portraying a soldier doing various types of KP duty, such as peeling potatoes and scrubbing pots.

SUPPLY LIST

- Jacquard towel in the color combination of your choice
- For the Tea Cup and Garden Tool towels, 3 skeins of DMC® floss that match the color in your towel
- For the Teapot towel, 1 skein of matching floss

DIRECTIONS

- Transfer the designs to the tea towel, using the light box and pen method. Refer to the Transferring Your Designs to Fabric section, page 10.
- Referring to the Embroidery Stitches section, page 11, embroider the designs, using 2 strands of floss.

French knots

Favorite Redwork Designs / Betty Alderman

French knot

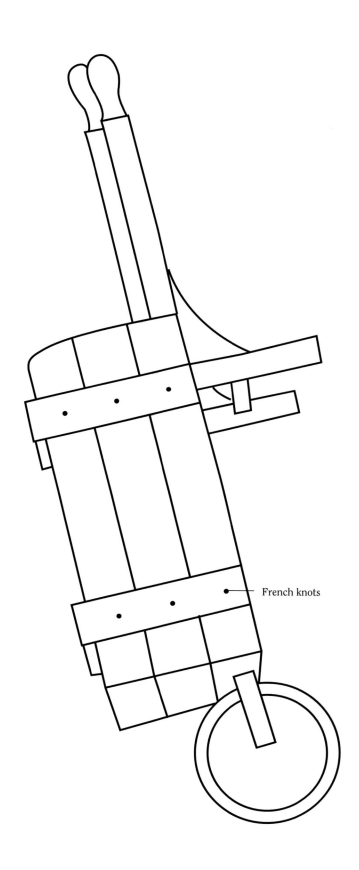

French knots

SUNBONNET FLOWER SHOW – REDWORK QUILT

40½" x 40½"

Sunbonnet Flower Show

The Sunbonnet twins have decided to enter a flower show. They water their seeds and gather their flowers. Lo-and-behold, their efforts win them a first-prize ribbon. Quilts that tell stories are great fun to make. One of these SUNBONNET FLOWER SHOW quilts is embroidered in the redwork tradition and set on point. Bright primary colors give a different look to the little four-block SUNBONNET FLOWER SHOW quilt. Directions for both settings are given.

SUPPLY LIST, REDWORK QUILT

- 5 skeins of DMC® floss, floss 498
- 1⅛ yds. light background fabric
- 1 yd. sashing and binding fabric
- ¼ yd. inner border fabric
- ⅝ yd. outer border fabric
- 44" x 44" backing fabric
- 44" x 44" batting

CUTTING MEASUREMENTS, REDWORK QUILT

BACKGROUND: Cut 5 squares, 10½" x 10½"
Cut 2 squares, 8" x 8", then cut the squares in half diagonally (Fig. 13a).
Cut 1 square, 15½" x 15½", then cut the squares in quarters diagonally (Fig. 13b).

SASHING: Cut 8 strips, 1¼" x 10½".
Cut 2 strips, 1¼" x 33½".
Cut 2 strips, 1¼" x 12".

INNER BORDER: Cut 2 strips, 1¼" x 31".
Cut 2 strips, 1¼" x 32½".

OUTER BORDER: Cut 2 strips, 4¾" x 32½".
Cut 2 strips, 4¾" x 41".

As stated in the General Directions section, the following lengths are guidelines. Be sure to measure your own quilt to determine the exact length of your sashings and borders.

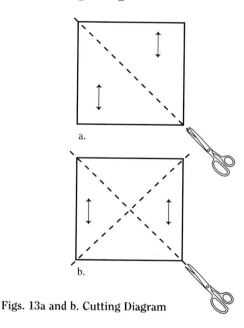

Figs. 13a and b. Cutting Diagram

DIRECTIONS, REDWORK QUILT

- Transfer all 5 of the SUNBONNET FLOWER SHOW designs to the background squares by the method you prefer. Be sure to place the design on the fabric so that it will be straight when the squares are place on point. Refer to the Transferring Your Designs to Fabric section, page 10.
- Embroider the Sunbonnet designs, using a stem stitch (Fig. 1, page 11), unless otherwise indicated. Use 2 strands of floss. *Note: The corner motifs will be embroidered after the quilt is assembled.*

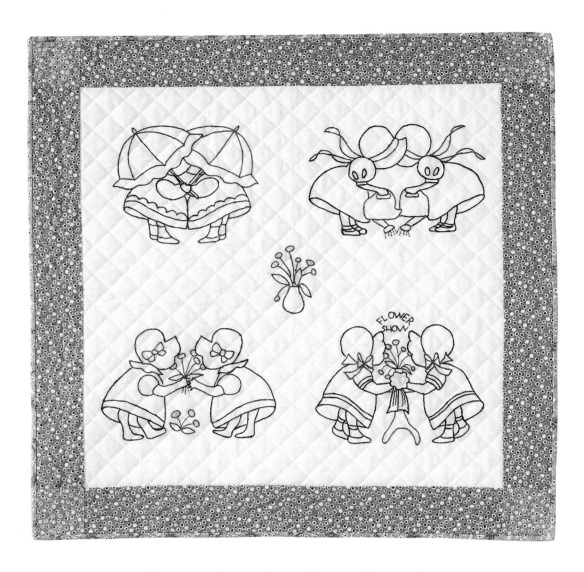

SUNBONNET FLOWER SHOW – PRIMARY COLORS QUILT

24" x 24"

Favorite Redwork Designs / Betty Alderman

Fig. 14. SUNBONNET FLOWER SHOW Layout Guide

- Assemble the quilt, referring to the SUNBONNET FLOWER SHOW layout guide (Fig. 14).
- After the quilt has been assembled, transfer the corner motif design, page 45, to the corners of each block and to the corners of the triangles.
- Embroider around each corner motif, using a buttonhole stitch (Fig. 3, page 11). Use 2 strands of floss.
- Refer to the General Directions section, page 9, for finishing your quilt.

SUPPLY LIST, PRIMARY COLORS QUILT

- 2 skeins of DMC® floss, blue 312
- 1 skein each of the following DMC® floss:
    Green 700
    Red 321
    Yellow 726
- ½ yd. light background fabric
- ¼ yd. border fabric
- ⅛ yd. corner-set fabric
- ¼ yd. binding fabric
- 28" x 28" backing fabric
- 28" x 28" batting

CUTTING MEASUREMENTS, PRIMARY COLORS QUILT

BACKGROUND: Cut 4 squares, 10½" x 10½".
BORDERS: Cut 4 strips, 2½" x 20½".
CORNER SETS: Cut 4 squares, 2½" x 2½".

DIRECTIONS, PRIMARY COLORS QUILT

- Transfer numbers 1, 2, 3, 4, and 5 of the SUNBONNET FLOWER SHOW designs (the flower vase design is transferred and embroidered after the quilt is assembled) to the background squares by the method you prefer. Refer to the Transferring Your Designs to Fabric section, page 10.
- Embroider, using a stem stitch (Fig. 1, page 11), unless otherwise indicated. Use 2 strands of floss.
- Assemble, using the PRIMARY COLORS layout guide (Fig. 15).
- Transfer the flower vase design to the center of the quilt. Embroider the design as you did the other designs.
- Refer to the General Directions section, page 9, for finishing your quilt.

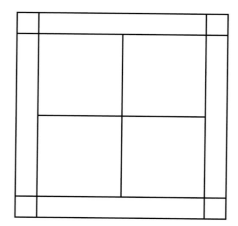

Fig. 15. PRIMARY COLORS Layout Guide

Sunbonnet Flower Show

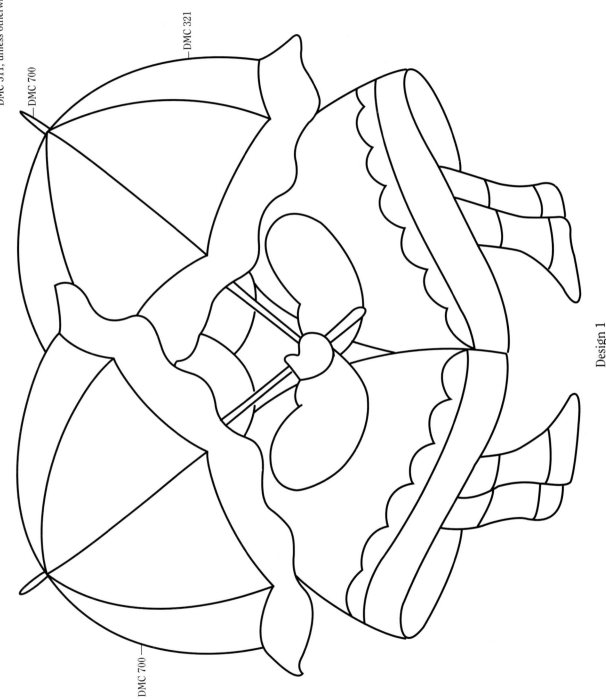

DMC 311, unless otherwise marked

DMC 700

DMC 321

DMC 700

Design 1

Favorite Redwork Designs / Betty Alderman

Sunbonnet Flower Show

DMC 311, unless otherwise marked

DMC 321

DMC 700

Design 2

DMC 700

DMC 321

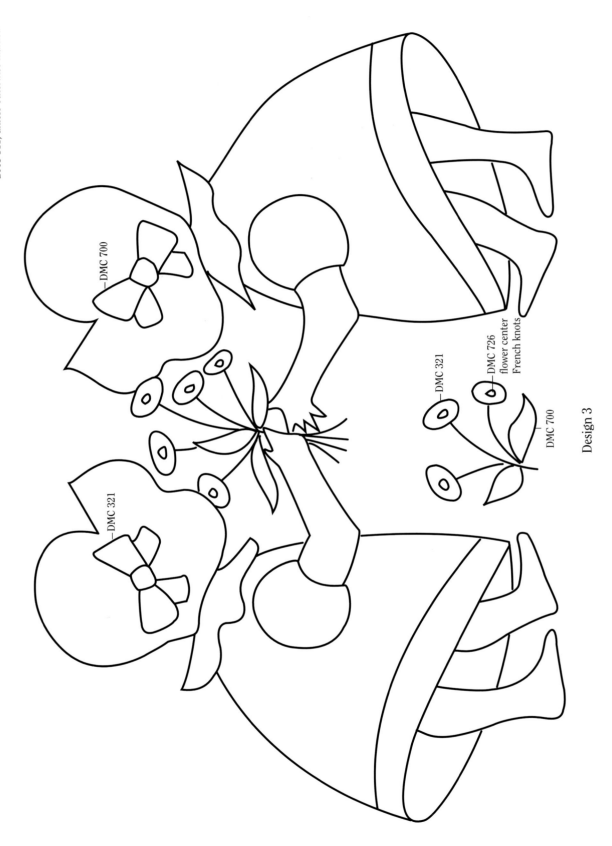

DMC 311, unless otherwise marked

DMC 700

DMC 321

DMC 321

DMC 726
flower center
French knots

DMC 700

Design 3

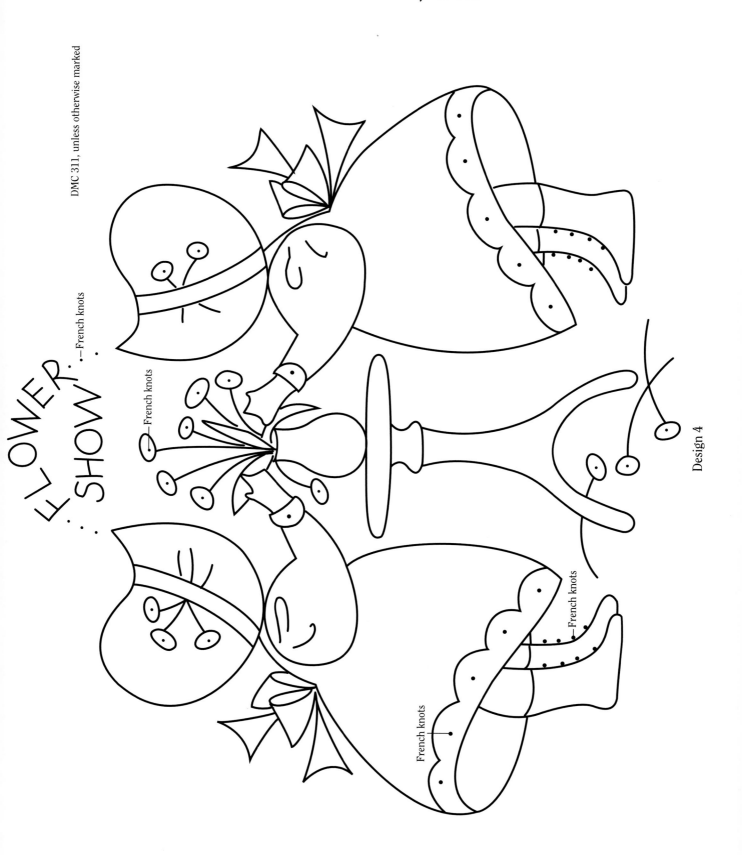

FLOWER SHOW

French knots

French knots

French knots

French knots

DMC 311, unless otherwise marked

Design 4

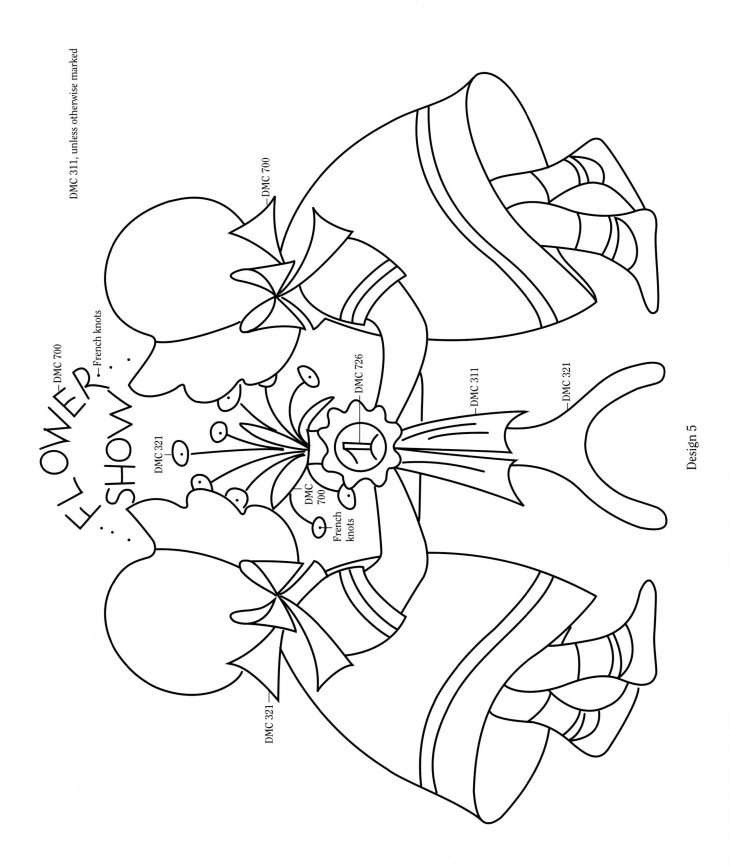

DMC 311, unless otherwise marked

DMC 700

FLOWER
SHOW
DMC 700
French knots

DMC 321

DMC 726

DMC 700
French knots

DMC 311

DMC 321

DMC 321

Design 5

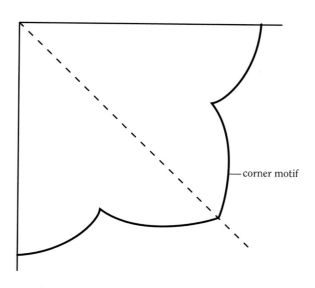

corner motif

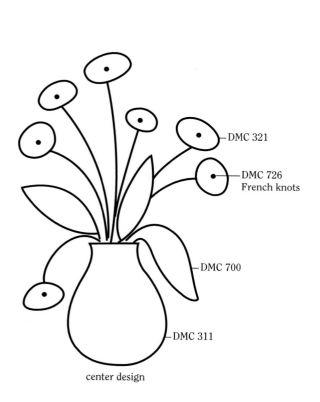

DMC 321

DMC 726
French knots

DMC 700

DMC 311

center design

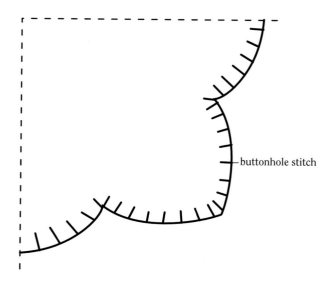

buttonhole stitch

FRIENDS AT MY GARDEN GATE

28½" x 28½"

Friends at My Garden Gate

Beyond my garden gate, more things abound than flowers and other forms of plant life. Dozens of living creatures make their home among the profusion of plants and, I hate to say this, weeds! The borders on this quilt depict just a few of the many interesting friends found in my own garden when I sit quietly and observe. You may question the inclusion of ducks in my redwork garden. My backyard has a brook running just behind a small hosta garden. Occasionally, I see ducks paddling along this little stream when the water is high after a heavy rain.

The printed fabric used in this quilt is called toile, pronounced twäl. Toile is a cotton or linen fabric, printed in just two colors. The printed design is usually an eighteenth-century pastoral scene, picturing men, women, children, and animals enjoying an idyllic country setting. I thought it was the perfect fabric to enhance the redwork embroidery of FRIENDS AT MY GARDEN GATE.

SUPPLY LIST

- 5 skeins of DMC® floss, red 498
- 1⅛ yd. light fabric for the background and border fabric
- ¾ yd. print fabric for triangles and binding
- 32" x 32" backing fabric
- 32" x 32" batting

CUTTING MEASUREMENTS

BACKGROUND: From the light fabric, cut the center square, 15½" x 15½".

LARGE TRIANGLES: From the print fabric, cut 2 squares, 12" x 12". Cut the squares in half, diagonally (Fig. 16).

You now have four large triangles. The triangles will be trimmed to the correct size after they have been applied to the center block.

BORDERS: From the light fabric, cut 4 strips, 4¼" x 22".

SMALL, CORNER TRIANGLES: From the light fabric, cut 2 squares, 5" x 5". Cut the squares in half diagonally (Fig. 16).

From the print fabric, cut 2 squares, 5" x 5". Cut the squares in half diagonally.

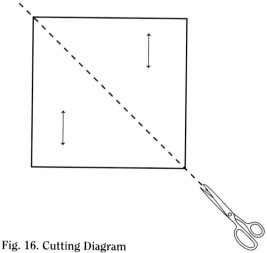

Fig. 16. Cutting Diagram

DIRECTIONS

- Transfer the FRIENDS AT MY GARDEN GATE design to the center square by the method you prefer. Be sure to place the design on the fabric so that it will be straight when the center square is set on point.
- Embroider the FRIENDS AT MY GARDEN GATE design, using the stem stitch and French knots shown in the Embroidery Stitches section, page 11. Use 2 strands of floss.

- Apply the long edge of each large triangle to the edges of the center square.
- Trim the resulting square to measure 22" x 22". There should be a ¼" seam allowance beyond the points of the embroidered square (Fig. 17).
- Make the border corners by sewing the small light triangles to the small print triangles on the long edges of the triangles (Fig. 18). Trim to 4¼" x 4¼".
- Add the borders and corner squares to the quilt center, referring to the FRIENDS AT MY GARDEN GATE layout guide (Fig. 19).
- Transfer 6 border motifs to each border. *Note: The top and bottom border is the same, although motifs are reversed.* The same is true of the side borders. Transfer the beetle motif to the corner squares.
- Embroider the border and corner motifs as you did the center square.
- Refer to the General Directions section, page 9, for finishing your quilt.

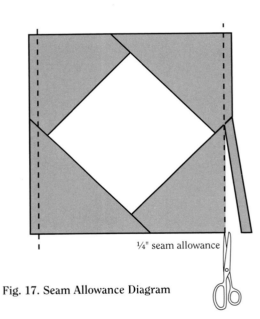

¼" seam allowance

Fig. 17. Seam Allowance Diagram

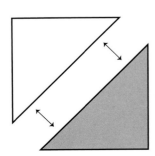

Fig. 18. Border Corners Diagram

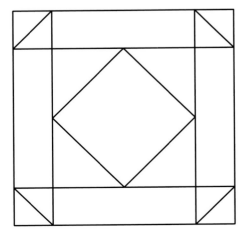

Fig. 19. FRIENDS AT MY GARDEN GATE Layout Guide

Friends at My Garden Gate

French knots

French knots

French knots

French knots

Favorite Redwork Designs / Betty Alderman

Friends at My Garden Gate

French knot

Favorite Redwork Designs / Betty Alderman

Friends at My Garden Gate

French knots—

French knots

French knot

French knots

French knots

French knots

Friends at My Garden Gate

French knots

French knots

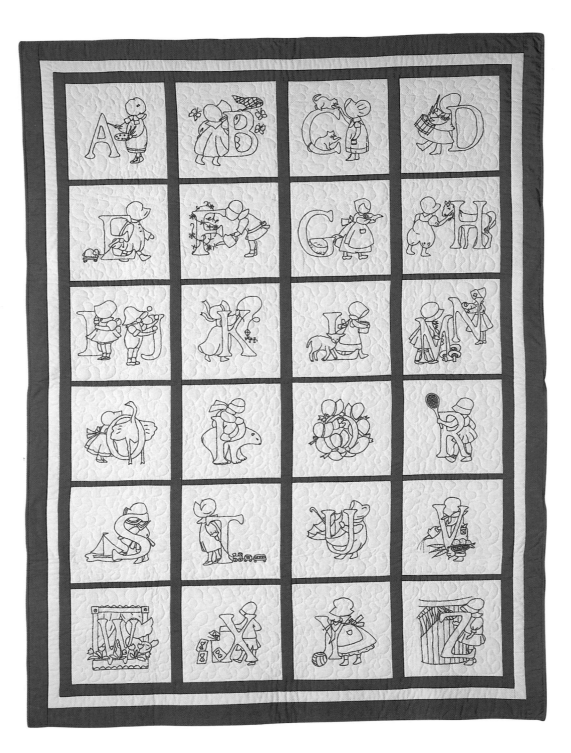

ALPHABET SUE
44" x 60½"

Favorite Redwork Designs / Betty Alderman

Alphabet Sue

The letters of the alphabet have made popular quilt blocks for many years. In fact, needle artists have incorporated the alphabet into their stitching for generations. Examples of early American samplers date from the middle of the seventeenth century. Young women learned their letters and how to execute them with thread and needle so that they might mark their household linens and other belongings. I have seen isolated examples of embellished letters executed in redwork, but have never personally seen an early quilt with the entire alphabet embroidered on it. I keep looking and hope to someday find such a treasure to be a companion to my alphabet quilt.

It was great fun designing these patterns. I hope you will easily see the connection between the characters and their letters. The letter X was a challenge, but you might like my solution. In case you haven't figured it out, it is a Xerox copy machine reproducing little sunbonnets.

The letters I and J have been condensed onto one block and the letters M and N onto another because I thought a 24-block quilt would be easier to design than a quilt containing 26 blocks. I'm sure you will find a lot of uses for these Sunbonnet letters of the alphabet.

SUPPLY LIST

- 8 skeins of DMC® floss, red 304
- 2 yds. light background fabric
- 2 yds. red sashing, border, and binding fabric
- 49" x 66" backing fabric
- 49" x 66" batting

CUTTING MEASUREMENTS

BACKGROUND: From the remaining light background fabric, cut 24 blocks, 9" x 9".

HORIZONTAL SASHING: From the red fabric, cut 20 strips, 1" x 9".

VERTICAL SASHING: From the red fabric, cut 3 strips, 1½" x 54". (Notice that the vertical sashing is wider than the horizontal sashing.)

INNER BORDER: From the red fabric, cut 2 strips, 1½" x 37½" (top and bottom). Cut 2 strips, 1½" x 56" (sides).

MIDDLE BORDER: From the light background fabric, cut 2 strips, 1½" x 39½" (top and bottom). Cut 2 strips, 1½" x 58" (sides).

OUTER BORDERS: From the red fabric, cut 2 strips, 2" x 41½" (top and bottom). Cut 2 strips, 2" x 61".

DIRECTIONS

- Transfer the designs to the 24 background blocks.
- Embroider the designs using 2 strands of floss. Most of the designs require the stem stitch. Dots indicate a French knot. The flowers on the letter F are done with a lazy daisy stitch. All stitch descriptions are found in the Embroidery Stitches section, page 11.
- Assemble the quilt, using the ALPHABET SUE layout guide (Fig. 20).
- Refer to the General Directions section, page 9, for finishing your quilt.

Fig. 20. ALPHABET SUE Layout Guide

Favorite Redwork Designs / Betty Alderman

Alphabet Sue

French knots

Alphabet Sue

French knots

Favorite Redwork Designs / Betty Alderman

French knots

French knots

Alphabet Sue

French knots

Favorite Redwork Designs / Betty Alderman

Alphabet Sue

French knots

Alphabet Sue

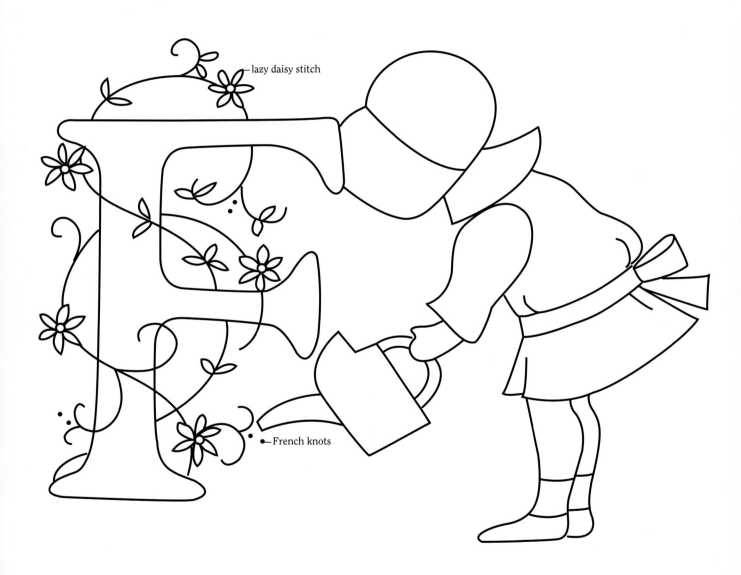

lazy daisy stitch

French knots

Favorite Redwork Designs / Betty Alderman

Alphabet Sue

Alphabet Sue

Favorite Redwork Designs / Betty Alderman

Alphabet Sue

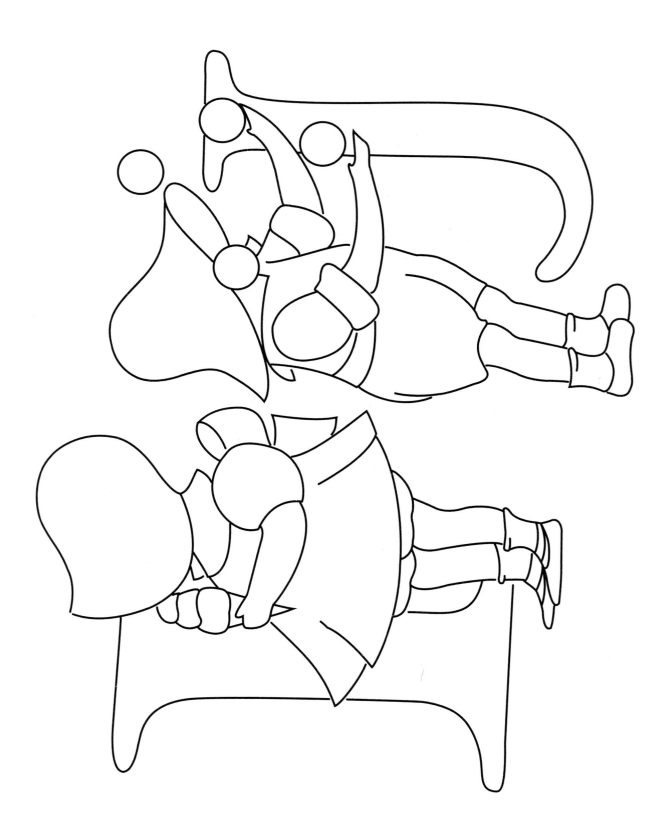

Alphabet Sue

Alphabet Sue

French knot

Alphabet Sue

Alphabet Sue

Favorite Redwork Designs / Betty Alderman

Alphabet Sue

French knots

Favorite Redwork Designs / Betty Alderman

Alphabet Sue

French knots

Favorite Redwork Designs / Betty Alderman

Alphabet Sue

French knots

Alphabet Sue

Favorite Redwork Designs / Betty Alderman

BOTANICAL REDWORK

39½" x 45½"

Botanical Redwork

The flowers in this quilt pay tribute to the young ladies of long ago who practiced their drawing skills depicting botanical specimens. During the latter part of the eighteenth century and throughout the nineteenth century, there was great interest in our biological surroundings. Drawing flowers and plant life in detail was considered a worthwhile and instructional pastime. We often find embroidered flowers and plants on redwork quilts from the late 1800s and early 1900s. Books on botany were also popular, and one can speculate that many of these redwork designs were traced from drawings found in these beautifully illustrated books of the time.

Among my collection of early redwork embroidery, there is a Jacquard woven tea towel. It has charming red-and-white woven designs on the edges and a very elaborate embroidered design in the middle. The red and white weaving is done in such a way that a lovely, soft, muted red is the result. The red and white tablecloth fabric that I chose for the sashing and inner border of this quilt is woven in just such a way that one part of the weave produces the same lovely color. That is the part used in the sashing. Whenever I look at this quilt, I am reminded of the beautiful red-and-white Jacquard tablecloths, napkins, and tea towels our great-grandmothers used on their tables and in their kitchens.

SUPPLY LIST

- 8 skeins of DMC® floss, red 321
- 2⅓ yds. white-on-white background and border fabric
- 1 yd. red and white tablecloth check for the sashing, inner border, and bias binding
- 44" x 50" backing fabric
- 44" x 50" batting

CUTTING MEASUREMENTS

BACKGROUND: Cut 9 rectangles, 8½" x 10½".

SASHING: Cut 6 strips, 1½" x 8½".
Cut 2 strips, 1½" x 32½".

INNER BORDER: Cut 2 strips, 2½" x 26½".
Cut 2 strips, 2½" x 36½".

OUTER BORDER: Cut 2 strips, 5¼" x 30½".
Cut 2 strips, 5¼" x 46".

DIRECTIONS

- Transfer the 9 BOTANICAL REDWORK designs to the background rectangles by the method you prefer. Refer to the Transferring Your Designs to Fabric section, page 10.
- Embroider the flower designs, using a stem stitch (Fig. 1, page 11) unless otherwise indicated. Use 2 strands of floss.
- Assemble the quilt, using the BOTANICAL REDWORK layout guide (Fig. 21).

- After the borders have been applied, transfer the border design onto them.
- Embroider, using a buttonhole stitch (Fig. 3, page 11) around the outline of the design. Use 2 strands of floss.
- Refer to the General Directions section, page 9, for finishing your quilt. Cut corner curves before binding.

Fig. 21. BOTANICAL REDWORK Layout Guide

Chinese Lantern

French knots

Christmas Rose

Daffodil

French knots

Daisy

French knots

Dandelion

Iris

French
knots

Sunflower

French knots

Thornapple

Waterlily

Botanical Redwork

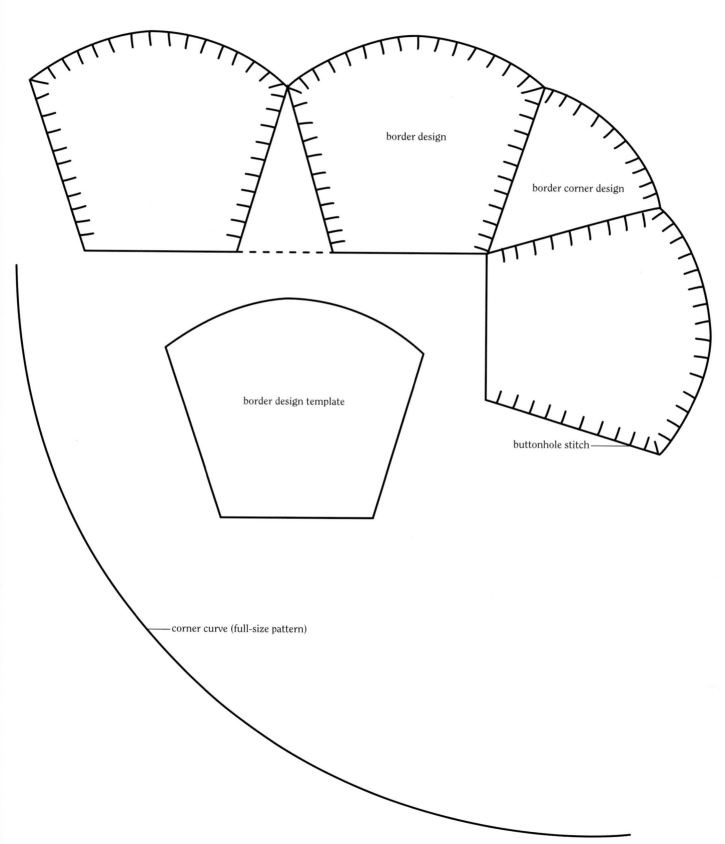

border design

border corner design

border design template

buttonhole stitch

corner curve (full-size pattern)

Sources

DMC® embroidery floss, quilt-basting spray starch, and monofilament thread are available at most quilt and fabric shops.

Jacquard tea towels are available at William-Sonoma, Inc., and K-Mart stores.

Bibliography

BEAL, STEPHEN. *The Very Stuff: Poems on Color, Thread, and the Habits of Women*. Interweave Press, Loveland, CO, 1995.

BUNNEY, SARAH, ED. *The Illustrated Encyclopedia of Herbs: Their Medicinal and Culinary Uses*. Chancellor Press, London, 1992.

VERMA, LOIS MARILYN, "What's New & News in Quilting Around the World: Botanicals Bloom in Nebraska," *Quilter's Newsletter Magazine*. Vol. 3, No. 3, Issue 311, Page 12, April 1999.

WEISSMAN, JUDITH REITER, AND WENDY LAVITT. *Labors of Love: America's Textiles and Needlework, 1650–1930*. Knopf, New York, NY, 1994.

Suggested Reading

ANDERSON, CLARITA S. *Figured & Fancy: Weavers of Wayne County, New York*. Wayne County Historical Society, Lyons, NY, 1996.

ATKINS, JACQUELINE MARX. *Shared Threads: Quilting Together Past and Present*. Viking Studio Books, New York, NY, 1994.

ELBERT, E. DUANE, AND RACHEL KAMM ELBERT. *History from the Heart: Quilt Paths across Illinois*. Rutledge Hill Press, Nashville, TN, 1993.

FROST, HELEN YOUNG, AND PAM KNIGHT STEVENSON. *Grand Endeavors: Vintage Arizona Quilts and their Makers,* First ed. Northland Publishing Company, Flagstaff, AZ, 1992.

GOLDMAN, MARILYN, AND MARGUERITE WIEBUSCH, et.al. *Quilts of Indiana: Crossroads of Memories/The Indiana Quilt Registry Project*. Indiana University Press, Indianapolis, IN, 1991.

HOLSTEIN, JONATHAN. *Kentucky Quilts*. The Kentucky Quilt Project Inc., Louisville, KY, 1982. Third printing, 1992.

MONTANO, JUDITH BAKER. *Elegant Stitches: An Illustrated Stitch Guide & Source Book of Inspiration*. C&T Publishing, Lafayette, CA, 1995.

SAFFORD, CARLETON L., AND ROBERT BISHOP. *America's Quilts and Coverlets*. Bonanza Books, New York, NY, 1985.

SINEMA, LAURENE. *Redwork Quilts and More*. Design Originals, Fort Worth, TX, 1999.

WARREN, ELIZABETH V., AND SHARON L. EISENSTAT. *Glorious American Quilts: The Quilt Collection of the Museum of American Folk Art*. Penguin Books USA Inc., New York, NY, 1996.

Biography

Betty's designs culminate from a background beginning with a fine arts education at Syracuse University, ownership of a yarn shop where she also designed needlepoint canvases, to the buying and selling of antique quilts while she was living in central Ohio. Her inspiration is derived from her past knowledge, her continued enthusiasm, and current research for her quilt pattern business, Betty Alderman Designs.

One of Betty's first quilts was a full-size, red, white, and blue Sherman's March quilt made in the mid-1970s for her son, Jim. Through the 1970s, Betty continued quilting and painting needlepoint canvases.

During the mid-1980s, Betty's husband, Fred, took a job in Phoenix, Arizona. She began working at The Quilted Apple, a well-known Phoenix-area quilt shop. The Quilted Apple allowed Betty the opportunity to stretch her creative talents in quiltmaking and pattern design. Betty taught quilting at The Quilted Apple and assisted with, and created, designs to be sold in the shop. Betty continued to sharpen her quilting skills, all the while developing a deep fondness for particular patterns and quilt types. Of those were the appliqué quilts of the last century and the Sunbonnet quilts of the twentieth century.

Around 1990, Betty and Fred moved to the city of Mansfield, Ohio. Betty became experienced in buying and selling antique quilts. From 1990 to 1995, Betty developed her antique business, supplying booths at antique malls with quilts bought at farm auctions throughout central Ohio.

Redwork quilts were often offered for sale at the auctions and Betty became interested in this type of quilt. In 1992, Betty created her first commercial pattern. Since then, redwork has become a significant part of her growing pattern business.

Back in her hometown of Palmyra, New York, Betty takes every opportunity to attend local auctions in search of those special antique quilts with which she is so enamored. While Betty occasionally teaches classes, most of her time is spent expanding her business by designing new patterns, introducing approximately eight to ten new patterns each year. For a look at Betty's patterns, visit her website at: http://www.LewisWritingServices.com/betty.

Other AQS Books

This is only a small selection of the books available from the American Quilter's Society. AQS books are known worldwide for timely topics, clear writing, beautiful color photos, and accurate illustrations and patterns. The following books are available from your local bookseller, quilt shop, or public library.

#5640   US$16.95

#5763   US$21.95

#5760   US$18.95

#5013   US$14.95

#5845   US$21.95

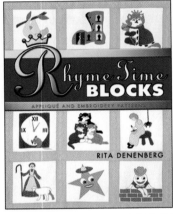

#5711   US$19.95

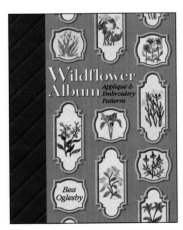

#5757   US$19.95

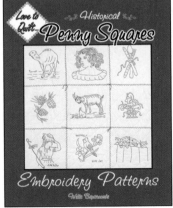

#4753   US$12.95

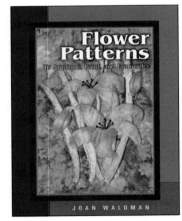

#5238   US$19.95

Look for these books nationally or call 1-800-626-5420